5-MINUTE GRATITUDE JOURNAL
FOR TEEN BOYS

5-MINUTE GRATITUDE JOURNAL FOR TEEN BOYS

Prompts for Wisdom, Courage, and Confidence

Lauren Blanchard Zalewski

ROCKRIDGE
PRESS

For general information on our other products and services or to obtain technical support, please contact our Customer Care Department within the United States at (866) 744-2665, or outside the United States at (510) 253-0500.

Rockridge Press publishes its books in a variety of electronic and print formats. Some content that appears in print may not be available in electronic books, and vice versa.

Interior and Cover Designer: Tricia Jang
Art Producer: Sara Feinstein
Editor: Maxine Marshall
Production Editor: Ruth Sakata Corley
Production Manager: Riley Hoffman

Author photo courtesy of Dorothy Salvatori Photography

Paperback ISBN: 978-1-63878-073-1
R0

I dedicate this book to all those who choose to walk toward infinite hope and joy by taking the path of gratitude. And to Rob, my lifelong walking partner, for giving me more reasons to be grateful than I could ever write.

"When you're grateful
for everything you have,
it just leads to happiness."

—DWAYNE "THE ROCK" JOHNSON

This Journal Belongs To:

_____

YOU GOT THIS

Hey guys, get ready to discover the power of gratitude. You might be wondering, "What is gratitude?" or "What's all the hype about?" The good news is that it's really quite simple.

Gratitude is about changing our perspective and looking at life through the lens of appreciation. We can rewire our brains to a default happiness setting simply by shifting how we focus on things. Gratitude journaling helps us become more aware of the good already in our lives. When we write things down, they are amplified to give us a clearer picture of where we are and where we'd like to go in the future.

Gratitude empowers us to take charge of our own happiness. Through the simple act of recording the "good stuff," we can reduce our stress, boost our joy, and energize our lives. What you hold here in your hands is an incredibly powerful tool that puts YOU in charge of regulating your own emotions and strengths.

I've worked with teens for many years, and I can appreciate the many different challenges that you face today. Today's teens experience more stress than ever, with so much pressure to excel at high levels. Social media adds to these anxieties. The good news is that by deepening your glimpse into the positive aspects of your life, you will be more prepared to handle challenges as they come your way.

I am excited to embark on this journey with you as you feel the way gratitude will improve your relationships and add an extra boost of joy and confidence to your life.

An Attitude of Gratitude

At first, getting started on your gratitude journey might seem a bit overwhelming. Just like muscles grow and strengthen with exercise, gratitude does the same. The more you practice it, the easier it gets and the stronger you become.

Studies show that by committing to gratitude, you can actually train your brain to think more positively, maintain better relationships with your friends and family, and build better confidence.

Need proof? At the University of California, more than 1,000 9th and 10th graders were assigned to do various gratitude practices, including spending 10 minutes each week writing letters of gratitude to people like their parents, coaches, and friends. After just one month, these students became happier, more motivated, and felt more connected to their friends and family.

By recording things in a gratitude journal, you can build resilience, improve sleep, boost your immune system, and fight off feelings of anxiety and depression. The practice can even give you more energy and motivation.

Five minutes a day is all that it takes. Congratulations on choosing an attitude of gratitude.

How to Use This Journal

The most important thing to know is that this journal is broken up into bite-size exercises that will take no more than five minutes of your day.

Quick and easy prompts help you become aware of the incredible world you live in. Answer honestly and specifically, as no thoughts or feelings are too small—no emotion is too intense or "wrong."

Along with each day's practice, you will find a quote selected to bring you inspiration. Each one was chosen to help you embrace positive feelings, boost your self-esteem, rid yourself of negative thoughts, and thrive in the now while reducing anxiety about the future.

Concluding each entry is a positive affirmation to help boost your confidence and enable you to access your new superpower of resilience. With resilience, you can go through life with strong decision-making abilities and the tools you need to help build your emotional "muscle."

Throughout the journal, you will find pages to pause and reflect on how gratitude is impacting your life. You will also find fun and attainable gratitude challenges that will help supercharge the benefits even further.

I have no doubt that as you go through this journal for just a few minutes each day, you will begin to see positive changes in your life, in your feelings, and in your relationships.

Let's get started!

Gratitude Goals

What are your goals for completing this journal? By setting your intentions up front, you'll be able to see the big picture more clearly. You'll be able to put your finger on the end result and get there more efficiently. Simply put, writing down your goals helps you stick to a plan and get to where you want to be faster.

By completing this journal, I hope to feel _____

_____

I believe that through writing down my thoughts and feelings, I will

begin to feel more _____

and less _____

because _____

One area where I am struggling is _____

_____

By incorporating gratitude into my life, I believe I can strengthen

_____

because _____

*"Give thanks. Appreciate what you do have . . . the more
we give thanks, the more we receive to be thankful for.
Gratitude is the gift that always gives back."*

—MATTHEW McCONAUGHEY

Something simple that I take for granted is _____

_____

_____

I am grateful for this simple thing because _____

_____

_____

I would feel _____

if I could no longer enjoy this simple pleasure because _____

_____

_____

Something I can do to appreciate this gift more is _____

_____

_____

I am grateful for the gifts that life provides me.

"Focusing on one thing that you are grateful for increases the energy of gratitude and rises the joy inside yourself."

—OPRAH WINFREY

A quality that I appreciate about myself is _____

_____

_____

I am grateful for it because _____

_____

_____

Over the years this quality has changed because _____

_____

_____

I can use this trait to make others happy by _____

_____

_____

I trust in my unique abilities.

*"The trick is to be grateful when your mood is high
and graceful when it is low."*

—RICHARD CARLSON

A song that always puts me in a good mood is _____

_____

_____

When I listen to it, I feel _____

_____

_____

What I like the most about this song is _____

_____

_____

A way I can keep this song available for when I need a "mood

reboot" is _____

_____

_____

I find joy in simple things.

"We must find time to stop and thank the people who make a difference in our lives."

—JOHN F. KENNEDY

A teacher or role model who has impacted my life is _____

_____

_____

A lesson they taught me that I am grateful for is _____

_____

_____

I can use this lesson throughout my life by _____

_____

_____

I can show my appreciation to this person by _____

_____

_____

I freely accept help and wisdom from others in order to grow.

DATE _____ / _____ / _____

"There are only two ways to live your life. One is as though nothing is a miracle. The other is as though everything is a miracle."

—ALBERT EINSTEIN

A skill that I am good at is _____

_____

_____

To master it, I had to _____

_____

_____

When I use this ability, I feel _____

_____

_____

A person I should thank for teaching me this is _____

_____

_____

I am grateful for my persistence.

"Sometimes it takes only one act of kindness and caring to change a person's life."

—JACKIE CHAN

An instance when someone gave me something they knew I really

needed was _____

_____

_____

When I received it, I felt _____

_____

_____

I think the reason they did this for me was _____

_____

_____

I was able to show them how grateful I was by _____

_____

_____

My life matters.

DATE _____ / _____ / _____

"You can't laugh and be afraid at the same time—of anything."

—STEPHEN COLBERT

Something that makes me laugh is _____

_____

_____

I am able to find things to laugh about when I _____

_____

_____

Someone who appreciates my sense of humor is _____

_____

_____

I am grateful for laughter in my life because _____

_____

_____

Laughter brings joy and relaxation into my life.

"If more of us valued food and cheer and song above hoarded gold, it would be a merrier world."

—J. R. R. TOLKIEN

One of my favorite foods is _____

_____

_____

When I enjoy it, I feel _____

_____

_____

If this food was no longer available to me, I would feel _____

_____

_____

I am grateful to _____

for making it possible for me to enjoy it.

I take time to savor the delicious food that nourishes me.

*"If you know who you are, it takes all the power
away from that negativity."*

—SELENA GOMEZ

I experienced peer pressure when _____

_____

_____

When it happened, I reacted by _____

_____

_____

The result of this experience was _____

_____

_____

My gratitude practice can help me stay true to myself by _____

_____

_____

I trust my judgment to know what is in my best interest.

*"It is not joy that makes us grateful; it is gratitude
that makes us joyful."*

—DAVID STEINDL-RAST

Stress makes an impact on my life when _____

_____

_____

When I am stressed, my mood affects my _____

_____

_____

In the past, I have reduced my stress by _____

_____

_____

I can use gratitude to help me with stress by _____

_____

_____

I can move past negative thoughts and use them as growth opportunities.

PAUSE *AND* REFLECT

How am I feeling today?

I feel this way because _____

_____

With my gratitude practice, I have noticed _____

_____

_____

I am learning that my gratitude practice can provide me with the tools I need to _____

_____

_____

Gratitude Challenge

When you are thinking about today's responsibilities or chores, replace the words "I *have* to" with "I *get* to." Notice if your perspective changes and, if so, how. For example, you might feel a sense of appreciation rather than obligation.

"This is a wonderful day. I've never seen this one before."

—MAYA ANGELOU

My favorite time of the day is _____

_____

_____

What makes this particular time special to me is _____

_____

_____

Some things I enjoy doing during this time are _____

_____

_____

I can appreciate this time of the day even more by _____

_____

_____

Today, I am energetic and overflowing with good feelings.

"The grass may be greener on the other side,
but the water bill is higher."

—TYLER PERRY

I sometimes feel as though I don't measure up to others when

_____

_____

I wish I could be more like them because _____

_____

_____

When I feel this way, I normally deal with it by _____

_____

_____

I can use this feeling to boost my own abilities by _____

_____

_____

I embrace all parts of me, including my imperfections.

"Abundance is not something we acquire.
It is something we tune into."

—WAYNE DYER

Something I want is _____

Something I need is _____

As I get older, I find myself wanting more things like _____

because _____

_____

_____

When I desire something, an action I take to get it is _____

_____

_____

I can use my gratitude practice to release some of my wants by

_____

_____

I have everything I need inside me and can tap into
gratitude whenever I want.

DATE _____ / _____ / _____

"Comedy is acting out optimism."

—ROBIN WILLIAMS

An embarrassing moment that made me take life less seriously was

_____

_____

When it happened, I felt _____

_____

_____

It helped me appreciate the lighter side of life by _____

_____

_____

A lesson from this that I'm grateful for is _____

_____

_____

It is okay to laugh at myself.

"We learned about gratitude and humility, that so many people had a hand in our success, from the teachers who inspired us to the janitors who kept our school clean—and we were taught to value everyone's contribution and treat everyone with respect."

—MICHELLE OBAMA

My favorite subject in school is _____

_____

_____

I like this subject because _____

_____

_____

The three things I love the most about this class are _____

_____

_____

It adds value to my life because _____

_____

_____

I am focused and disciplined.

"It's up to us to choose contentment and thankfulness now—and to stop imagining that we have to have everything perfect before we'll be happy."

—JOANNA GAINES

Someone who inspires me with their positive attitude is _____

_____

_____

One of the things I admire most about them is _____

_____

_____

I have witnessed them overcoming difficult situations by _____

_____

_____

I can follow their example by _____

_____

_____

My path is paved toward greatness.

"Happiness is itself a kind of gratitude."

—JOSEPH WOOD KRUTCH

Something I like to do with my downtime is _____

_____

_____

I can fully appreciate these moments by _____

_____

_____

Somebody I enjoy doing this with is _____

_____

_____

An action I can take to create more of this downtime is _____

_____

_____

I take time to breathe so I can reboot.

"If you count all your assets, you always show a profit."

—ROBERT QUILLEN

A quality that an ideal friend would possess is _____

_____

_____

This appeals to me because _____

_____

_____

A quality that I possess that makes me a good friend is _____

_____

_____

Something I can do to be a better friend is _____

_____

_____

I am thankful for my friends and for the chance to be a friend to others.

"Remember that what you now have was once among the things you only hoped for."

—EPICURUS

A talent of mine that I am grateful to have is _____

_____

_____

I first realized that I had this talent when _____

_____

_____

To become so skilled at it, I had to _____

_____

_____

Others appreciate this talent of mine because _____

_____

_____

I learn and grow by trying new things.

*"You have to grab moments when they happen.
I like to improvise and ad-lib."*

—DENZEL WASHINGTON

If I knew today was my last day on earth, something I would want to

try is _____

_____

_____

Someone who I would want to spend this day with would be _____

_____

_____

Something I would want my loved ones to know is _____

_____

_____

I would want to be remembered as _____

_____

_____

I have the ability to do what brings me joy.

PAUSE AND REFLECT

How am I feeling today?

I feel this way because _____

_____

With my gratitude practice, I have noticed _____

_____

_____

Something I have learned not to take for granted is _____

_____

_____

Gratitude Challenge

As you sit down for your next meal, take the time to consider
what it took for that food to get to your plate. Think of the people
involved in the process, starting from the grower of the food right
down to the chef, family member, or friend who may have prepared
the meal for you. Share your appreciation with the people in your
household who were involved in the process.

*"I am happy because I'm grateful. I choose to be grateful.
That gratitude allows me to be happy."*

—WILL ARNETT

My favorite genre of movie is _____

_____

_____

What I like most about this type of movie is _____

_____

_____

I was introduced to this genre by _____

_____

_____

Something I have learned about myself based on my love for this

kind of movie is _____

_____

_____

I make time for fun, fulfilling activities.

"Sacrifice is a part of life. It's supposed to be. It's not something to regret. It's something you aspire to."

—MITCH ALBOM

A time when someone sacrificed something to help me was _____

_____

_____

In order to help me, they gave up _____

_____

_____

Knowing that they cared enough about me to make this sacrifice

makes me feel _____

_____

_____

I showed them my appreciation by _____

_____

_____

I am worthy of love and grateful for those who love me.

*"Because when you stop and look around,
this life is pretty amazing."*

—DR. SEUSS

Something wonderful in my surroundings at this very moment is

_____

_____

I am grateful for it because _____

_____

_____

Something I just discovered through observation, which I never

noticed before, is _____

_____

_____

I can become more mindful of my surroundings in the future by

_____

_____

I feel safe and secure within myself.

"As a child, I didn't know what I didn't have. I'm thankful for the challenges early on in my life because now I have a perspective on the world and kind of know what's important."

—AMERICA FERRERA

I was given a second chance when _____

_____

_____

The first time didn't go so well because _____

_____

_____

I changed things the second time around by _____

_____

_____

I am grateful for this second chance because _____

_____

_____

I am not perfect, and that is okay.

DATE _____ / _____ / _____

"Gratitude is when memory is stored in the heart and not in the mind."

—LIONEL HAMPTON

Something I'd like to remember forever is _____

_____

_____

I am grateful for this memory because _____

_____

_____

My perception of this memory has evolved in the way _____

_____

_____

Something I can do to make sure this stays on my "gratitude radar"

forever is _____

_____

_____

I hold the power to turn negative thoughts into positive beliefs.

"We can only be said to be alive in those moments when our hearts are conscious of our treasures."

—THORNTON WILDER

If I could travel anywhere in the world, I would go to _____

_____

_____

This place appeals to me because _____

_____

_____

I learned about this place by _____

_____

_____

A visit there would bring me joy because _____

_____

_____

I am a magnet for great opportunities.

DATE _____ / _____ / _____

"Gratitude is a currency that we can mint for ourselves and spend without fear of bankruptcy."

—FRED DE WITT VAN AMBURGH

A habit that I would like to change is _____

_____

_____

It negatively impacts my life by _____

_____

_____

Something that motivates me to change it is _____

_____

_____

An action I can take to break this habit is _____

_____

_____

I am powerful and can do hard things.

*"When I started counting my blessings,
my whole life turned around."*

—WILLIE NELSON

I am different today than I was one year ago because _____
_____
_____

I have grown as a person by _____
_____
_____

A quality that I've developed over this past year that I am grateful
for is _____
_____
_____

During this year, something I learned about myself is _____
_____
_____

I am grateful for change in my life and am open to new possibilities.

"If you get up in the morning and think the future is going to be better, it is a bright day. Otherwise, it's not."

—ELON MUSK

A recent success that I had was _____

_____

_____

For this to happen, I had to _____

_____

_____

I celebrated this achievement by _____

_____

_____

An action I can take to allow for more wins like this in the future is

_____

_____

I achieve amazing things.

"Education is the most powerful weapon which you can use to change the world."

—NELSON MANDELA

Something I would like to learn is _____

_____

_____

I first became interested in this when _____

_____

_____

Something I could do to learn more about it is _____

_____

_____

Learning this would enrich my life by _____

_____

_____

I am open to learning new things.

PAUSE AND REFLECT

How am I feeling today?

I feel this way because _____

_____

With my gratitude practice, I have noticed _____

_____

_____

Something surprising that I am now finding myself grateful for is

_____

_____

Gratitude Challenge

Before going to bed tonight, quickly write a list of five things
that made you grateful today. You may think of exciting things
to write down or you may also think of simpler things like clean
drinking water or your home for the shelter it provides you. Use
your imagination!

*"The service you do for others is the rent you pay
for your room here on Earth."*

—MUHAMMAD ALI

A way that someone made my life better today was _____

_____

_____

It made me grateful because _____

_____

_____

I was able to show them my appreciation by _____

_____

_____

I can "pay it forward" by _____

_____

_____

I am grateful for those who have helped me.

"Trophies and medals have never meant much to me. I've had amazing experiences, which let you feel like you've accomplished something."

—JOHN KRASINSKI

One of the best experiences of my life was _____

_____

_____

I am grateful that it happened because _____

_____

_____

When it happened, I remember feeling _____

_____

_____

Something special I will always remember about it is _____

_____

_____

I take time to appreciate life's adventures as they happen to me.

"Things won't go perfect. It's all about how you adapt from those things and learn from mistakes."

—MICHAEL PHELPS

A challenging situation that brought out the best in me was

_____

_____

It was challenging because _____

_____

_____

I surprised myself with my strength by _____

_____

_____

I am grateful for this challenge because _____

_____

_____

I have the strength to handle struggles that come my way.

"Instead of trying to fit an impossible ideal, I took a personal inventory of all my healthy body parts for which I am grateful."

—TINA FEY

Something small but mighty that my body can do is _____

_____

_____

I feel challenged by my body when _____

_____

_____

My body is important to me because _____

_____

_____

I can show more appreciation for the things my body *can* do by

_____

_____

I am thankful for each breath I take.

*"Look around, look around at how lucky we are
to be alive right now."*

—LIN-MANUEL MIRANDA

A good night's sleep helps me to _____

_____

_____

At bedtime, I am fortunate that I have _____

_____ as shelter.

Something that makes me comfortable when I sleep is _____

_____

_____

One nighttime ritual I value is _____

_____

_____

Sleep restores me and gives me the power
I need to tackle each day.

DATE _____ / _____ / _____

"The tiniest change in perspective can transform a life."

—OPRAH WINFREY

Something I am looking forward to tomorrow is _____

_____

_____

I am excited about it because _____

_____

_____

Somebody who is making this possible for me is _____

_____

_____

I will appreciate this moment by _____

_____

_____

My confidence will enable me to make tomorrow a great day.

"What you're supposed to do when you don't like a thing is change it. If you can't change it, change the way you think about it. Don't complain."

—MAYA ANGELOU

Something I complain about is _____

_____

_____

I complain about it because _____

_____

_____

When I complain, it leaves me feeling _____

_____

_____

Something I can do to shift my perspective is _____

_____

_____

If I can't change a situation, I can change my attitude instead.

"Surround yourself with good people. People who are going to be honest with you and look out for your best interests."

—DEREK JETER

The person I am most comfortable talking to is _____

_____

_____

I am comfortable with them because _____

_____

_____

When they are listening to me, I feel _____

_____

_____

I can show them my appreciation by _____

_____

_____

I have people I can count on in my life who believe in me.

*"We make a living by what we get;
we make a life by what we give."*

—WINSTON CHURCHILL

The last time I helped someone who was struggling was _____

_____

_____

I felt the need to help them because _____

_____

_____

Giving them the help they needed made me feel _____

_____

_____

Something I will always remember from the experience is _____

_____

_____

I have many strengths to offer others.

"Gratitude is the key to happiness. If you have a healthy understanding of gratitude, you can't lose."

—CHRIS EVANS

Someone famous who inspires me is _____

_____

_____

The thing I admire most about them is _____

_____

_____

I am grateful for what they teach me because _____

_____

_____

I can learn from their example by _____

_____

_____

I can be great.

PAUSE AND REFLECT

How am I feeling today?

I feel this way because _____

_____

With my gratitude practice, I have noticed _____

_____

_____

I used to think gratitude was _____. Now I recognize

that gratitude has the power to _____.

Gratitude Challenge

Recognize one ungrateful thought that you have today and turn it around into a grateful one. Try applying this to various situations throughout the day and notice how your perspective changes.

Example:

Ungrateful thought: "My parent is nagging me about doing my homework again. I wish they would leave me alone."

Grateful thought: "My parent cares enough about me to want to see me do my best in school. They do this because they love me."

"Cultivate the habit of being grateful for every good thing that comes to you, and to give thanks continuously. And because all things have contributed to your advancement, you should include all things in your gratitude."

—RALPH WALDO EMERSON

When something doesn't go as I expected, I often react by _____

_____

_____

For me, "going with the flow" looks like _____

_____

_____

Change makes me feel _____

_____

_____

I feel grateful for change when _____

_____

_____

Obstacles strengthen my character and give me a broader perspective on the world.

"Creativity is intelligence having fun."

—ALBERT EINSTEIN

One way I show my creative side is _____

_____

_____

Being creative makes me feel _____

_____

_____

I share my creations with _____

_____

_____

Creativity makes the world _____

_____

_____

There are no limits to my creativity.

"Failure is so important. We speak about success all the time. It is the ability to resist failure or use failure that often leads to greater success. I've met people who don't want to try for fear of failing."

—J. K. ROWLING

Failing at something makes me feel _____

_____

_____

If I wasn't afraid to fail, I would _____

_____

_____

I want to do this because _____

_____

_____

I can boost my courage by _____

_____

_____

If I fail, I can use the experience to grow.

*"Everything has its wonders, even in darkness
and silence, and I learned, whatever state I may be in,
therein to be content."*

—HELEN KELLER

Out of the five senses, the one I am most grateful for is _____

_____

_____

This sense brings me joy because _____

_____

_____

If I no longer had use of this sense, I would feel _____

_____

_____

I can savor this sense more by _____

_____

_____

There are lots of ways for me to engage with the world.

*"Kindness is the language which the deaf
can hear and the blind can see."*

—MARK TWAIN

A random act of kindness I received once was _____

_____

_____

When it happened, I felt _____

_____

_____

It surprised me because _____

_____

_____

One way I can give back to others is _____

_____

_____

I appreciate kind gestures, large and small.

"The most important thing, in anything you do, is always trying your hardest, because even if you try your hardest and it's not as good as you'd hoped, you still have that sense of not letting yourself down."

—TOM HOLLAND

My dream job would be _____

_____

_____

This job would allow me to _____

_____

_____

I would be great at it because _____

_____

_____

I could impact people by _____

_____

_____

I have unlimited potential.

"I stay positive by actually choosing things to be thankful for. An attitude of gratitude literally gives you energy."

—TERRY CREWS

Something others admire about me is _____

_____

_____

The reason they admire it is _____

_____

_____

The fact that they like this about me makes me feel _____

_____

_____

I am grateful to have this characteristic because _____

_____

_____

I am proud of the person I see in the mirror.

"The only approval you need is your own."

—AMANDA GORMAN

One time I stuck up for myself was when _____

_____

_____

I felt the need to advocate for myself because _____

_____

_____

After I did it, I felt _____

_____

_____

I was grateful that I took the initiative because _____

_____

_____

I am strong and capable of standing up for myself.

DATE _____ / _____ / _____

*"Those who are happiest are those who do
the most for others."*

—BOOKER T. WASHINGTON

Somebody in my family who does a lot for me is _____

_____

_____

I am grateful for them because _____

_____

_____

Some of the things they do for me are _____

_____

_____

I can show my appreciation by _____

_____

_____

It makes me more powerful to accept
help when I need it.

"Sometimes we get so caught up in our daily lives that we forget to take the time out to enjoy the beauty in life."

—KEANU REEVES

Something I cherish in nature is _____

_____

_____

I value it because _____

_____

_____

I notice it most when _____

_____

_____

I can take more time to appreciate it by _____

_____

_____

I am grateful for my senses that allow me to enjoy the beauty around me.

PAUSE AND REFLECT

How am I feeling today?

I feel this way because _____

_____

With my gratitude practice, I have noticed _____

_____

_____

By focusing on gratitude, I see a change in my _____

_____

_____

Gratitude Challenge

Take a walk outside and look at everything as if you were a toddler seeing things in nature for the first time. Pay close attention to every detail. Think about how a child might experience a sense of wonder about something you take for granted. Use your "gratitude radar" to gain a new appreciation for the beauty found in nature.

"Folks are usually about as happy as they make their minds up to be."

—ABRAHAM LINCOLN

Something that went right for me today was _____

_____

_____

I set myself up for success by _____

_____

_____

What made it a "win" for me was _____

_____

_____

When things go well for me during the day, it affects my attitude by

_____

_____

I love the person I am becoming.

DATE _____ / _____ / _____

"Gratitude is the closest thing to beauty
manifested in an emotion."

—MINDY KALING

My ideal day would be _____

_____

_____

I would enjoy it because _____

_____

_____

Something special that would make this day great would be

_____

_____

I could use my senses to appreciate this day by _____

_____

_____

I make the best out of each day.

"Enthusiasm is the electricity of life."

—GORDON PARKS

An invention that makes my life easier is _____

_____

_____

It helps me _____

_____

_____

I got it from _____

_____

_____

When I use this amazing invention, I can remind myself to be

thankful for it by _____

_____

_____

I can master anything I put my mind to.

"Don't let anyone tell you to change who you are."

—MARK ZUCKERBERG

The times I recognize my worth are when _____

_____

_____

This makes me unique from many others because _____

_____

_____

I can grow this strength by _____

_____

_____

I can use this valuable asset to help me in the future by _____

_____

_____

I am the only person on the planet like me.

"Don't cry about your past. Life is full of pain. Let the pain sharpen you, but don't hold on to it. Don't be bitter."

—TREVOR NOAH

Something that motivates me is _____

_____

_____

When I am motivated, it helps me _____

_____

_____

It makes me want to do better because _____

_____

_____

I am grateful when I accomplish my goals because _____

_____

_____

I am ready, willing, and able to handle my responsibilities.

"The earlier you learn that you should focus on what you have and not obsess about what you don't have, the happier you will be."

—AMY POEHLER

Something I am looking forward to in the future is _____

_____

_____

I am excited for this to happen because _____

_____

_____

When it happens, my life will improve because _____

_____

_____

The thing I will be the most grateful for about it is _____

_____

_____

I am excited about the future.

"Your time is limited, so don't waste it living someone else's life."

—STEVE JOBS

A hobby of mine that I am grateful for is _____

_____

_____

I first became interested in it when _____

_____

_____

I can learn more about this hobby by _____

_____

_____

The thing I love the most about it is _____

_____

_____

My hobbies and talents make my life rewarding.

DATE _____ / _____ / _____

"It's not possible to experience constant euphoria, but if you're grateful, you can find happiness in everything."

—PHARRELL WILLIAMS

Happiness, to me, is _____

_____

_____

Being happy is important because _____

_____

_____

I am able to bring happiness to others by _____

_____

_____

A way that gratitude helps boost my happiness is _____

_____

_____

I have the power to bring happiness to my life.

"I'm continually trying to make choices that put me against my own comfort zone. As long as you're uncomfortable, it means you're growing."

—ASHTON KUTCHER

I feel uncomfortable when _____

_____

_____

I have dealt with this situation in the past by _____

_____

_____

I can learn to make these situations more comfortable by _____

_____

_____

Situations like this have taught me that _____

_____

_____

All of my problems have solutions.

"What separates privilege from entitlement is gratitude."

—BRENÉ BROWN

A time I was lucky was _____

_____

_____

I considered myself fortunate because _____

_____

_____

This fortunate situation made me feel _____

_____

_____

I can better savor these moments of luck by _____

_____

_____

I appreciate all the good things that come my way.

PAUSE AND REFLECT

How am I feeling today?

I feel this way because _____

_____

With my gratitude practice, I have noticed _____

_____

_____

An area of my life that is improving with gratitude is _____

_____

_____

Gratitude Challenge

To supercharge your gratitude today, ask yourself these
four questions:
- What did I learn today?
- What or who inspired me today?
- What made me smile today?
- What was my favorite thing that happened today?

"Since I'm not sure of the address to which to send my gratitude, I put it out there in everything I do."

—MICHAEL J. FOX

A new beginning that I am grateful for is _____

_____

_____

I am thankful for it because _____

_____

_____

I can make the best of this new opportunity by _____

_____

_____

I can share my appreciation for it by _____

_____

_____

I am grateful for new beginnings and new opportunities.

"Gratitude is a way of seeing that alters our gaze."

—DR. ROBERT A. EMMONS

Someone showed me compassion when _____

_____

_____

They offered it to me because _____

_____

_____

Their compassion made me feel _____

_____

_____

I am grateful that people care about me because _____

_____

_____

I have people who care about me and want me to succeed.

*"I know a lot of people who have a lot of everything, and
they're absolutely the most miserable people in the world.
So it won't do anything for you unless you're a happy
person and can have peace with yourself."*

—LENNY KRAVITZ

My most prized possession is _____

_____

_____

It is special to me because _____

_____

_____

I received it when _____

_____

_____

I take care of this possession by _____

_____

_____

**My belongings are a bonus, but everything
I need lies within me.**

"No matter what happens in life, be good to people. Being good to people is a wonderful legacy to leave behind."

—TAYLOR SWIFT

The best gift I've ever given someone is _____

_____

_____

I gave it to them because _____

_____

_____

Giving them this gift made me feel _____

_____

_____

They showed their appreciation by _____

_____

_____

Giving to others boosts my own gratitude.

"Every time we feel satisfied with what we have, we can be counted as rich, however little we may actually possess."

—ALAIN DE BOTTON

Something that worries me is _____

_____

_____

I worry about it because _____

_____

_____

I have gotten through this worry by _____

_____

_____

I can change my thinking by _____

_____

_____

I am focused on my success, not my worries.

"I acknowledge my feeling and gratitude for life by praising the world and whoever made all these things."

—MARY OLIVER

I am grateful for my bedroom because _____

_____

_____

My favorite part about it is _____

_____

_____

When I am in my room, I feel _____

_____

_____

I can show my appreciation for having a place to sleep by _____

_____

_____

I do my best to appreciate and care for my surroundings.

"Showing gratitude is one of the simplest yet most powerful things humans can do for each other."

—RANDY PAUSCH

A time when someone thanked me was _____

_____

_____

They shared their appreciation because _____

_____

_____

When someone thanks me for something, I feel _____

_____

_____

Being thanked inspires me to give more because _____

_____

_____

I have so much to give, and I do so freely.

"Instead of looking for what's wrong with everything, I started to look for what was right with everything."

—TERRY CREWS

I feel special because _____

_____

_____

The best part about being me is _____

_____

_____

I work hard to be the best person I can be by _____

_____

_____

Being grateful makes me even better by _____

_____

_____

I am my own superhero.

"The heart that gives thanks is a happy one, for we cannot feel thankful and unhappy at the same time."

—DOUGLAS WOOD

I am grateful for my family because _____

_____

_____

What makes us unique is _____

_____

_____

My family helps me _____

_____

_____

I can show them I appreciate them by _____

_____

_____

I have a solid foundation to build the life that I want.

"The only way to make sense out of change is to plunge into it, move with it, and join the dance."

—ALAN WATTS

I had to be brave when _____

_____

_____

I needed to find my courage because _____

_____

_____

When it was happening, I felt _____

_____

_____

When I recognized I was being brave, I felt _____

_____

_____

I am strong and capable.

PAUSE AND REFLECT

How am I feeling today?

I feel this way because _____

_____

With my gratitude practice, I have noticed _____

_____

_____

I am sharing my gratitude more openly by _____

_____

_____

Gratitude Challenge

Pick an object that will encourage you to feel grateful each time you look at it. It can be a small item that reminds you of something you love, like a baseball if you love sports or a pen if you love to write or draw. Place your object in a spot you look at frequently—each time you see it, it will prompt you to be grateful for all that you have in your life.

"There are going to be times where you will have bad days, bad weeks, and even sometimes bad months, but rainbows always come after the darkest storm."

—DEMI LOVATO

A piece of good news I received recently was _____

_____

_____

I was grateful for this news because _____

_____

_____

When I get good news, I feel _____

_____

_____

I shared this good news with _____

_____

_____

I have the power to make my dreams come true.

"Everything can be taken from a man but one thing: the last of the human freedoms—to choose one's attitude in any given set of circumstances, to choose one's own way."

—VIKTOR E. FRANKL

Something I find interesting is _____

_____

_____

What interests me about it is _____

_____

_____

I am grateful for this interest because _____

_____

_____

I can use this interest to improve my life by _____

_____

_____

I am in charge of my life, and I choose happiness.

"At the age of 18, I made up my mind to never have another bad day in my life. I dove into an endless sea of gratitude from which I never emerged."

—PATCH ADAMS

Being my age is great because _____

_____

_____

Each year, things get better in my life because _____

_____

_____

Something good that I didn't expect to have at this age is _____

_____

_____

I can enjoy and appreciate the current moment by _____

_____

_____

There is no one better to be than myself.

"Embrace the void and have the courage to exist."

—DANIEL HOWELL

Life would be boring without _____

_____

_____

I am grateful for it because _____

_____

_____

It makes my life better by _____

_____

_____

I can create fun experiences by _____

_____

_____

I can create and control my own happiness.

*"It's our choices that show what we truly are,
far more than our abilities."*

—J. K. ROWLING

The best decision I ever made was _____

_____

_____

It was a great decision because _____

_____

_____

It affected my life in a positive way by _____

_____

_____

I have learned from this experience by _____

_____

_____

I am confident in my choices.

DATE ____ / ____ / ____

"Don't let the sun go down without saying thank you to someone, and without admitting to yourself that absolutely no one gets this far alone."

—STEPHEN KING

My favorite book is _____

_____

_____

This book is special because _____

_____

_____

After reading it, I felt _____

_____

_____

A lesson I have taken from it is _____

_____

_____

I build my wisdom and strength every day.

"Small things can lead to huge changes, and if those changes end up being obstacles, try to learn from them instead of letting them crush you."

—JOEY GRACEFFA

I was surprised or caught off guard when _____

_____

_____

At first, this change made me feel _____ because

_____

_____

It changed the way I live my life by _____

_____

_____

I am grateful for this experience because _____

_____

_____

I am open to life's unexpected twists and turns. They are chances to grow.

> *"Let us be grateful to people who make us happy; they are the charming gardeners who make our souls blossom."*

—MARCEL PROUST

The best gift I ever received was _____

_____

_____

It was given to me by _____ because _____

_____

_____

What I love most about this gift is _____

_____

_____

I thanked the person who gave it to me by _____

_____

_____

I surround myself with people who treat me well.

"Someone told me a few months ago to wake up first thing in the morning and think of three things or people I am grateful for. I've been doing that lately— nice way to start the day."

—JIMMY CHIN

A small thing that I do to take care of myself each day is _____

_____

_____

I do this because _____

_____

_____

Someone or something that helps me do this is _____

_____

_____

If I left this out of my daily routine, I would feel _____

_____

_____

I am grateful for my body, and I take good care of it.

DATE _____ / _____ / _____

*"I looked around and thought about my life. I felt grateful.
I noticed every detail. That is the key to time travel. You can
only move if you are actually in the moment."*

—AMY POEHLER

The aspect of my town or city that I am most grateful for is _____

_____

_____

It is special because _____

_____

_____

I would describe the best parts about where I live to someone who

just moved here by saying _____

_____

_____

I can appreciate it more by _____

_____

_____

I am grateful for my community.

PAUSE AND REFLECT

How am I feeling today?

I feel this way because _____

_____

With my gratitude practice, I have noticed _____

_____

_____

Gratitude gives me power by _____

_____

_____

Gratitude Challenge

Write yourself a letter as if it were from someone who knows and loves you (like a best friend or a family member). In the letter, list five reasons they would say they are grateful for you and what makes you special to them. Write your letter with compassion, as if you were writing to your own best friend.

"When nobody else celebrates you, learn to celebrate yourself. When nobody else compliments you, then compliment yourself."

—JOEL OSTEEN

A way that I make myself proud is _____

_____

_____

I am able to do this because _____

_____

_____

Through doing this, I have learned _____

_____

_____

I can continue to do this by _____

_____

_____

I am building my future one day at a time.

"Live a life full of humility, gratitude, intellectual curiosity, and never stop learning."

—GZA

Something useful that I learned recently is _____

_____

_____

I learned it by _____

_____

_____

It is interesting because _____

_____

_____

I can apply this to my life by _____

_____

_____

It is okay to make mistakes. I learn from each one I make.

*"The deepest craving of human nature is
the need to be appreciated."*

—WILLIAM JAMES

I am passionate about _____

_____

_____

It means a lot to me because _____

_____

_____

When I talk about it, I feel _____

_____

_____

I am grateful for this passion because _____

_____

_____

My positive thoughts create positive feelings.

"I think I learned to appreciate and treasure each day, because you don't know how many you're going to be given."

—SANDRA DAY O'CONNOR

Something that excites me about my life right now is _____

_____

_____

It is happening because _____

_____

_____

When I think about it, I feel _____

_____

_____

I can take the time to enjoy this by _____

_____

_____

Today is going to be my day.

"Gratitude is the single most important ingredient to living a successful and fulfilled life."

—JACK CANFIELD

I define success as _____

_____

_____

To me, that is success because _____

_____

_____

I work toward success in my life by _____

_____

_____

I am grateful for my successes because _____

_____

_____

I am capable of success.

"Living in a state of gratitude is the gateway to grace."

—ARIANNA HUFFINGTON

An area of my life that I would like to improve is _____

_____

_____

I'd like to boost it a bit because _____

_____

_____

An action I can take to improve it is _____

_____

_____

When I improve myself, I feel _____

_____

_____

I am ready, willing, and able to improve myself.

DATE _____ / _____ / _____

Something I can do to help myself today is _____

_____

_____

It would help me by _____

_____

_____

I will be grateful for this help because _____

_____

_____

I can motivate myself to take this action by _____

_____

_____

I am motivated, and I act when necessary.

"I used to be so convinced that happiness was the goal, yet all those years I was chasing after it I was unhappy in the pursuit. Maybe the goal really should be a life that values honor, duty, good work, friends, and family."

—ROBERT DOWNEY JR.

If I could choose one superpower, it would be _____

_____

_____

I would choose this because _____

_____

_____

I would use this power to improve my life by _____

_____

_____

The closest thing I currently have to a superpower is _____

_____

_____

I choose to be the best version of myself.

DATE _____ / _____ / _____

*"The meaning of life is to find your gift.
The purpose of life is to give it away."*

—PABLO PICASSO

A random act of kindness I can do for someone today is _____

_____

_____

I believe this would help them because _____

_____

_____

I enjoy giving and doing for others because _____

_____

_____

When people do kind things for me, it makes me feel _____

_____

_____

I can make the lives of others better
by offering kindness.

"Feeling gratitude and not expressing it is like wrapping a present and not giving it."

—WILLIAM ARTHUR WARD

If my life were made into a movie, it would be called _____

_____

_____

The actor who could best play me is _____

_____

_____

The general plot would be _____

_____

_____

I am grateful for my life story because _____

_____

_____

I am the hero of my own life's story.

PAUSE AND REFLECT

How am I feeling today?

I feel this way because _____

_____

With my gratitude practice, I have noticed _____

_____

_____

I have learned that gratitude is _____

It is not _____

Gratitude Challenge

Within the next day, take the time to compliment a stranger. Look for someone who has done something nice for you or who you feel has done a good job with something. Go out of your way to compliment them. Watch their reaction. How did they respond? How did it make you feel?

"Gratitude opens the door to the power, the wisdom, the creativity of the universe."

—DEEPAK CHOPRA

Something I enjoy collecting is _____

_____

_____

I began my collection when _____

_____

_____

I add to my collection by _____

_____

_____

I am grateful for this collection because it makes me feel _____

_____

_____

I am an original.

"When everything seems to be going against you, remember that the airplane takes off against the wind, not with it."

—HENRY FORD

Something I have struggled with recently is _____

_____

_____

I was able to get through this difficult time by _____

_____

_____

Something I learned that can help me turn around similar

struggles is _____

_____

_____

I'm grateful for this experience because _____

_____

_____

No matter what happens, I am equipped to handle it.

"Gratitude makes sense of our past, brings peace for today, and creates a vision for tomorrow."

—MELODY BEATTIE

Something that calms me is _____

_____

_____

When I am able to do this, I feel _____

_____

_____

I am grateful for calm moments because _____

_____

_____

I can apply this to stressful moments by _____

_____

_____

I am calm and can reboot during times of stress or anxiety.

"How wonderful it is that nobody need wait a single moment before starting to improve the world."

—ANNE FRANK

An impact I'd like to leave on the world is _____

_____

_____

I would like to gift this to the world because _____

_____

_____

I am the right person to offer this because _____

_____

_____

Leaving this impact would make me feel _____

_____

_____

I have the power to make the world a better place.

*"The roots of all goodness lie in the soil of
appreciation for goodness."*

—DALAI LAMA

A small thing that makes me happy is _____

_____

_____

I treasure it because _____

_____

_____

Without it, I would feel _____

_____

_____

I can use this to boost my happiness by _____

_____

_____

I see beauty in small and simple things.

"In the end, maybe it's wiser to surrender before the miraculous scope of human generosity and to just keep saying thank you, forever and sincerely, for as long as we have voices."

—ELIZABETH GILBERT

A way I would like to volunteer is _____

_____

_____

I would like to offer my service because _____

_____

_____

I could make a difference by _____

_____

_____

By offering my help in this area, I would feel _____

_____

_____

Giving to others enhances my own happiness.

"I don't have to chase extraordinary moments to find happiness—it's right in front of me if I'm paying attention and practicing gratitude."

—BRENÉ BROWN

Something I hope to accomplish this week is _____

_____

_____

I'd like to work toward this because _____

_____

_____

I can help myself reach this goal by _____

_____

_____

When I meet my goals, I feel _____

_____

_____

Anything is possible if I put my mind to it.

DATE _____ / _____ / _____

"Try and fail, but never fail to try."

—JARED LETO

Something I worked hard at and never gave up on was _____

_____

_____

I was determined to do this because _____

_____

_____

When it paid off, I felt _____

_____

_____

Something I learned about myself from this experience was

_____

_____

I can handle anything that comes my way.

"Of all the attitudes we can acquire, surely the attitude of gratitude is the most important and by far the most life-changing."

—ZIG ZIGLAR

Something I am determined to do in the future is _____

_____

_____

I am committed to this goal because _____

_____

_____

To achieve this, I will need to _____

_____

_____

I will be grateful to reach this goal because _____

_____

_____

I am determined and have the ability to reach my goals.

"If everything was perfect, you would never learn and you would never grow."

—BEYONCÉ

Something unusual that I am grateful for is _____

_____

_____

It is out of the ordinary because _____

_____

_____

I first discovered it by _____

_____

_____

I like it so much because _____

_____

_____

I am interesting.

PAUSE AND REFLECT

How am I feeling today?

I feel this way because _____

_____

With my gratitude practice, I have noticed _____

_____

_____

My _____ has changed for the better with my
gratitude practice.

Gratitude Challenge

Use your senses to observe your surroundings right now. What do
you see? Smell? Taste? Feel? Hear? What would be different if you
were to remove one of your senses, such as your sight or your hear-
ing? What would you miss?

"Not only do I think being nice and kind is easy, but being kind, in my opinion, is important."

—DWAYNE "THE ROCK" JOHNSON

The best compliment I ever received was _____

_____

_____

When I received it, I felt _____

_____

_____

It changed the way I view myself by _____

_____

_____

Kind words are important because _____

_____

_____

I am valued for what I offer the world.

"Acknowledging the good that you already have in your life is the foundation for all abundance."

—ECKHART TOLLE

Something I enjoy that I feel is underrated is _____

_____

_____

Others don't see the value in it because _____

_____

_____

It deserves more attention because _____

_____

_____

I can appreciate it more by _____

_____

_____

It is okay to be different.

DATE _____ / _____ / _____

"Don't count the days; make the days count."

—MUHAMMAD ALI

My favorite season is _____

_____

_____

I am grateful for it because _____

_____

_____

An activity that I enjoy during this season is _____

_____

_____

My favorite memory from this season is _____

_____

_____

Each day holds awesome possibilities.

*"Giving thanks for abundance is greater
than the abundance itself."*

—RUMI

I feel most generous when _____

_____

_____

I want to give more during this time because _____

_____

_____

When I am generous, it makes me feel _____

_____

_____

I was very generous when _____

_____

_____

I am generous and grateful for what I have to give.

"As we express our gratitude, we must never forget that the highest appreciation is not to utter words but to live by them."

—JOHN F. KENNEDY

I forgave someone when _____

_____

_____

They wronged me by _____

_____

_____

I chose to forgive them because _____

_____

_____

When someone forgives me, I feel _____

_____

_____

I forgive myself and others.

"Twenty years from now you will be more disappointed by the things you didn't do than by the ones you did."

—MARK TWAIN

I tried something new when _____

_____

_____

I tried it because _____

_____

_____

Doing new things makes me feel _____

_____

_____

A lesson from this experience that I am grateful for is _____

_____

_____

I am open to trying new things.

DATE _____ / _____ / _____

*"If you don't embrace the bad, you can never truly
embrace the good and be grateful and have gratitude
for the tiniest things."*

—SLOWTHAI

Something that made me sad was _____

_____

_____

When I am sad, I react by _____

_____

_____

During these times, I am comfortable sharing my feelings with

_____

_____

Gratitude can help me deal with sad feelings by _____

_____

_____

**My emotions are valid, and there is strength
in sharing them with others.**

*"Resolve to keep happy, and your joy and you shall
form an invincible host against difficulties."*

—HELEN KELLER

My "happy place" is _____

_____

_____

It is special to me because _____

_____

_____

When I am in this happy place, I feel _____

_____

_____

If I could no longer go there, the thing I would miss the most is

_____

_____

**I am grateful for safe places to
go when I need comfort.**

*"Piglet noticed that even though he had a Very Small Heart,
it could hold a rather large amount of Gratitude."*

—A. A. MILNE

A time I felt guilt over something was _____

_____

_____

The reason it made me feel guilty was because _____

_____

_____

Normally when I feel guilt or shame, I respond by _____

_____

_____

Something I can do to reduce my feelings of guilt is _____

_____

_____

I allow myself to move forward with life and am at peace with my past.

"A miracle happened: another day of life."

—PAULO COELHO

One action I can take right now to change my life for the better is

_____

_____

In order to do this, I need _____

_____

_____

My attitude of gratitude will help me by _____

_____

_____

I am motivated to do this because _____

_____

_____

An attitude of gratitude helps me live my best life possible.

Achievement Unlocked!

Journaling helped me achieve my goal of _____

_____

_____

_____

Gratitude taught me how to ease my struggles by _____

_____

_____

_____

Before starting this practice, I used to think
gratitude meant _____

_____

_____

_____

Now I understand gratitude can be used to _____

_____

_____

_____

ABOUT THE AUTHOR

 **Lauren Blanchard Zalewski** is a writer, speaker, passionate champion of all things gratitude, and self-diagnosed "gratitude addict"—hence the name of her blog. She is the founder of the Facebook group Attitude of Gratitude with Chronic Pain as well as its sister group, Attitude of Gratitude with Chronic Pain Journaling Club. Additionally, she hosts the weekly live broadcast "Gratefully Living the Chronic Life," which streams on both Facebook Live and YouTube.

Lauren is a voracious student of the human experience and has spent many years practicing intensive research into the power of gratitude as a tool for those who endure life's difficulties such as pain and illness. Her mission, passion, and life's work are in spreading the message of gratitude as the ultimate tool for resilience, hope, and joy even through the most difficult of circumstances. After working with teens for many years through the nonprofit community theater group she cofounded, she is excited to spread the message of gratitude for them to apply to their own unique struggles.

The mother of two grown children, Lauren lives in Hunterdon County, New Jersey, with her high school sweetheart husband, Rob, and Rory the Wondercat.

Follow her at GratitudeAddict.com.